THE LITTLE BOOK OF
WHISKY
TIPS

ANDREW LANGLEY

THE LITTLE BOOK OF
WHISKY
TIPS

ANDREW LANGLEY

A.

Absolute Press

Absolute Press
An imprint of Bloomsbury Publishing Plc

50 Bedford Square   1385 Broadway
London WC1B 3DP   New York NY 10018
UK   USA

www.bloomsbury.com
Absolute Press and the A. logo are trademarks of Bloomsbury Publishing Plc

First published in 2007.
Reprinted 2012, 2013, 2014 (twice).

A catalogue record for this book is available from the British Library.
Library of Congress Cataloguing-in-Publication data has been applied for.
ISBN 13: 9781904573654

Printed and bound in Spain by Tallers Gràfics Soler

'Always carry a large flagon of whisky in case of snakebite, and furthermore always carry a small snake.'

W.C. Fields

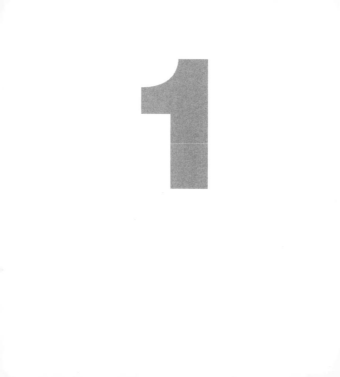

To get the **fullest aroma and flavour** of a whisky, **drink** it **from a tulip-shaped 'snifter' glass.**

Any whisky will benefit from this sort of respectful attention. As with wines, the narrow top of the glass will concentrate the aroma wonderfully. It will also encourage you to sniff and sip, rather than simply slurp.

2

Drink whisky any way you like.

There are a thousand different approaches to whisky drinking – with or without ice, water and a vast range of mixers – and none of them is definitively the right one. All the same, take the time occasionally to savour the drink in its simplest state – neat or with a little water.

3

For cocktails and other mixes, use one of the lighter whiskies.

A Canadian, a light Bourbon or a British blend with plenty of grain are best. Heavy malts tend to dominate the taste with their idiosyncratic – though magnificent – qualities.

4

Serve a good quality single malt at room temperature.

You can even warm the glass with your hands (a good reason for using a stemmed glass). This will gently release the volatile oils and other aromas. If the liquid is too cold, you will miss them.

5

When flaming a dish in whisky, always **heat the spirit** well through **first.**

Do this in a tiny saucepan or on a spoon (though very carefully if it's over a naked flame), then pour over and apply a match. Tepid whisky won't light. It will simply soak into the food and make it soggy.

6

A highball is the simplest and most famous of all whisky cocktails.

Simply a measure of whisky (Bourbon, Irish or blended Scotch) over ice in a tall glass, topped with soda water, it can be decorated with a twist of lemon peel. With rye whisky, use ginger ale instead of soda.

7

Coming down with a cold?

Try the classic Scots remedy –

a hot whisky toddy. Put a measure of whisky, plus the juice of half a lemon, in a glass. Top up with very hot water and stir in a large teaspoonful of honey. Drink as swiftly as possible.

8

High-quality Scotch whisky deserves high-quality water.

Tap water will do, as long as you let it stand for a while so that the chlorine can vapourize. However, a still spring water is free of added chemicals which might affect the taste (as is distilled water). Best of all, use burn water gathered near the distillery itself.

9

Before putting your

Seville orange marmalade

into its jars, stir in a shot or two of a blended

Scotch whisky.

Do this when the marmalade is still warm, otherwise it won't mix in. Resist the temptation to overdo the whisky – the taste comes through surprisingly strongly.

10

Whisky cream is a sensational accompaniment for mince pies.

Actually, that should read *whiskey* cream, because Irish whiskey is the best ingredient. Fold a teaspoon of icing sugar and a shot of whiskey into 225ml ($^1/_2$ pint) of whipped cream. Plonk on mince pies straight from the oven.

11

Should one add water to a good whisky?

Some drinkers like it neat, claiming that the delicate purities of aroma and flavour should not be diluted. However, a small amount of water (never more than equal to the liquor) will set off simple chemical reactions which release subtler aspects of both bouquet and taste.

12

Great Whisky Combinations No.1: Whisky and prawns.

Mix a shot of malt whisky with the same amount of ginger wine, plus a tablespoon of runny honey and some chopped fresh ginger. Use this to marinate 2 diced avocado pears and 8 ounces (225g) of peeled prawns for 30 minutes. Serve on lettuce with lemon slices.

13

Atholl brose

is an ancient and celebrated

Scotch whisky drink.

Mix 4 tablepoons of oatmeal with cold water until it becomes a paste. After 30 minutes, strain off the liquid. Mix 3 tablespoons of honey with 500ml (1 pint) of this oatmeal liquid, put into a wine bottle and fill up with malt whisky. Shake well and serve.

When you first pour a good whisky,

take time to study its appearance.

Swirl the liquid to coat the sides of the glass,

and examine the **colour and clarity** against the light. The shade of the whisky gives pleasure in itself, but also may provide clues about what vessel it has been aged ('matured') in.

15

At Hogmanay, it is permissible to **douse your haggis with a drop of whisky** from your glass. Purists may shudder, but the the tang of the malt combines perfectly with the pepperiness of the haggis. The better the Scotch, the better the taste.

16

Sazerac is **a sensational** – if eccentric – **whiskey cocktail from New Orleans.**

Stir together a teaspoon of sugar, a dash of Angostura bitters and a shot of rye whiskey. Strain into a glass and add a slug of Pernod or another pastis. Serve with a slice of lemon.

17

Spend some minutes smelling your single malt.

'Nose' plays a big part in the enjoyment of whisky. Put your nose into the top of the glass and sniff, gently at first. Try to identify the different aromas (flowers? seaweed? smoke? pine? honey? salt?). Swill the whisky and sniff again – you'll get something different this time.

18

If you make your own

Christmas puddings,

be sure to **add some whisky to the mix.** Put in one good shot for every pudding, but don't be tempted to overdo it. Too much liquid will stop the pud from cooking properly. The mixture should just drop from the spoon.

19

Scotch whisky and Scottish salmon are perfect partners.

Poach 6 salmon steaks. Whisk 3 egg yolks and the juice of a lemon, heating until it thickens in a bowl over boiling water. Stir in 125g (4oz) butter bit by bit. Remove from the heat and add a shot of whisky and an equal amount of poaching stock. Pour over the steaks.

20

On a cold winter's night,

warm yourself with a hot whisky punch.

Stick four cloves into a wedge of lemon.
Pop it into a heatproof glass with a big teaspoon
of sugar and a shot of whisky (blended Scotch
or Irish). The conventional finish is to top up with
hot water. An intriguing alternative is a weak
(milkless) Indian tea.

21

Great Whisky Combinations No.2: Whisky and Oranges.

Gently heat the juice of one orange with 12 tablespooons of brown sugar, a measure of whisky and an equal amount of water. When mixed, add 3 peeled and thinly sliced oranges and cook for two to three minutes. Chill and serve with cream.

22

Taste is, of course, at the heart of the whisky magic.

Take a sip and roll it round on your tongue. The spirit will simply evaporate in the mouth, but you should get the 'feel' of the whisky – an infinitely varied combination of sweet and dry, cream and pepper, smoke and honey. Dream up your own description.

23

Here's a variation on the much-loved Irish coffee

phenomenon, made in heaven to be poured on ice cream. Heat a syrup of 75ml (3fl oz) water and 225g (8oz) sugar gently until it caramelizes. Then stir in 225ml (8 fl oz) fresh-made coffee and let cool. Finally, add a measure of good Irish whiskey (no cream!).

24

If you build up a whisky collection, take the trouble to **store** your bottles safely. Store it **away from direct sunlight** (which can affect the colour of the spirit and bleach the label) and **in a cool, dry and stable place.** Unlike wine, whisky bottles can be kept upright: a little alcohol will vaporize and keep the cork moist.

25

Whisky often makes

an intriguing alternative to cognac or calvados

in meat dishes. Brown two veal escalopes and a cubed apple in butter, then flambe with a shot of warmed whisky until the flames die down. Stir in 150ml ($1/4$ pint) of single cream and cook gently for a couple of minutes. Serve with apples and sauce on top.

26

After sipping your whisky and feeling it in the mouth, **wait for the finish.** This consists of the flavours which arrive after the liquid itself has gone. These may include vanilla, wood and even salt, and may be long and warming or short and dry. **The longer** the finish, **the better** (and older) the whisky.

27

Japanese whisky can be

an astoundingly good – if expensive – accompaniment for Japanese food. This is especially true of sushi.

The malty flavours of the whisky marry well with the sweetness of soy sauce or miso, while its salty feel is echoed by the seafood and seaweed dishes.

28

The Whiskey Collins cocktail

is named after its inventor, the celebrated US bartender Tom Collins. In a shaker, blend some ice, a shot of Bourbon, the juice from 2 lemons and a teaspoon of powdered sugar. Strain into a glass. Add orange and lemon slices and top with a cherry. Straw advisable.

29

How long does a whisky last?

The short answer is – indefinitely, as long as it is sealed in an unopened bottle. Whisky is matured in oak casks, which allow it to breathe and develop. Once it is bottled, the breathing stops and the liquor goes into suspended animation. 'Laid down' bottles will not improve with age.

30

Great Whisky Combinations No.3: Whisky and Chocolate.

Put 6 crushed chocolate digestive biscuits in a dish. Whip up 500ml (1 pint) of sugared cream and a shot of whisky, then fold in 2 whipped egg whites. Lay the mixture over the crushed biscuits, and top with grated chocolate and toasted flaked almonds

31

Always read the label on the bottle.

This can tell you a lot. For instance, something called Scottish Whiskey (rather than Scotch Whisky) will probably be anything but. The label should also define whether it is 'Blended' (a mix of malt and grain whiskies), 'Malt Whisky' (a mix of malts) or 'Single Malt' (not mixed in any way).

32

A Rusty Nail

brings together

two great Scottish institutions.

Pour a shot of blended Scotch over ice in a tumbler. Then gently add a measure of Drambuie, pouring it over the back of a teaspoon so that it floats on top of the whisky.

33

Irish whiskey and seafood are made for each other.

Soften six sliced leeks in oil for 10 minutes. Remove, add more oil and sear two dozen scallops for 2 minutes a side. Removes these and degrease the pan with a shot of good Irish whiskey. Stir in 3 tablespoons of cream and pour over the leeks and scallops.

34

Here's **another surprising marriage of whisky and orange.** Place four slices each of peeled orange, peeled lemon and fresh pineapple in a blender. Whizz briefly then add a large measure of blended Scotch or bourbon and a generous dash of Orange Curacao and whizz again. Pour over ice.

35

For the legendary Manhattan cocktail,

a sweet vermouth is mixed with double the quantity of rye or bourbon whiskey. This is stirred with ice, strained into a glass and topped with a cherry. For a dry Manhattan – less well-known – substitute dry for sweet vermouth, and an olive for the cherry

36

Single malt whiskies usually have their **age stated on the label** (something like 'Aged 12 Years'). This indicates the time spent maturing in cask before bottling. Some bottles – confusingly – instead declare the distillation date and the bottling date. The age will be the difference between the two.

37

Does your whisky go hazy when you add water or ice?

Rejoice. You are drinking one of the few whiskies (such as the great Springbank) to have escaped chill filtration. This cosmetic process removes compounds which cause hazing. Some believe it also removes some of the whisky's special flavour and feel.

38

Jazz up pork or gammon steaks

with an Irish whiskey sauce. Fry four steaks in butter for 8 minutes a side. Remove and fry a chopped onion. Stir in 25g (1oz) of flour – slowly – and then 150ml ($\frac{1}{4}$ pint) of stock and a tablespoon of sugar. Finally bung in a measure of Irish whiskey, heat and pour over the steaks.

39

When it first comes from the still,

whisky is naturally colourless.

The colour of the bottled stuff usually comes from two sources. One is the wood in which the spirit is aged (new oak for bourbon, for example, or old sherry casks for some Scotches).
The other is – unromantically – sugar caramel.

40

Old Fashioned

is the name, but this

whiskey cocktail

has been in fashion for over a century. Put a lump of sugar in a short, squat glass and soak with a drop or two of Angostura bitters. Squash the sugar with a spoon and stir in a shot of rye or bourbon. Add ice and a twist of lemon peel.

How long does a bottle of whisky last once opened?

It depends on how much is left. When you open a bottle, you let in air. This immediately starts to react with the whisky, releasing volatile elements such as the alcohol and aromas. A near-empty bottle contains a lot of air, and will lose its 'edge' very swiftly.

42

Cauliflower cheese is transformed by a touch of whisky.

Blanch the florets for 5 minutes, drain and put in an ovenproof dish. Heat 300ml ($\frac{1}{2}$ pint) double cream, stirring in grated Cheddar cheese. Away from the heat, add a double shot of Scotch and a tablespoon of fine oatmeal. Pour over the cauliflower and bake for 45 minutes.

43

Great Whisky Combinations No.4: Whisky and Figs.

Gently poach some dried figs in water. Then drain and steep them in Irish whiskey for at least 24 hours. This heavenly marriage of tastes was invented by a descendant of Napoleon in the mid-nineteenth century.

44

A mint julep is the classic beverage for spectators of the Kentucky Derby.

Boil up a syrup of equal parts sugar and water. Cool and refrigerate overnight with a handful of fresh mint. Next day, put crushed ice in a julep cup and add a tablespoon of the mint syrup and a slug of Kentucky whisky. Stir and garnish with a sprig of mint.

45

Scottish island malts

such as a Lagavulin or an Ardbeg

go particularly well with blue cheese.

The smokiness of the peat and the iodine taste of the sea are a feisty match for the pungency of a Gorgonzola or a Roquefort. Better still, try a fine Scottish-produced cheese such as Lanarkshire Blue or Dunsyre Blue.

46

Whisky matures more quickly in hot climates.

Therefore spirit from warm regions such as the southern USA, India, Spain, Tennessee and Turkey will reach a drinkable age when comparatively young. Whiskies from colder places, such as New Zealand, Canada and of course Scotland will mature when rather older.

47

A whisky egg nog is a great pick-me-up

(known by Scots as 'Auld man's Milk'). Put ice, 240ml (8fl oz) milk, a double shot of blended Scotch, a raw egg and a teaspoon of sugar into a shaker. Shake energetically and pour into a glass. Grate some nutmeg on top and drink.

48

When planning your Christmas cake, remember to start the day before you bake. This gives you time to measure out the dried fruit and **soak it overnight in whisky.** This will plump it up and make the end result much moister – and tastier.

49

The Robbie Burns cocktail is a bizarre tribute to **Scotland's greatest poet** but he'd have loved it. Fill a cocktail shaker with ice, a shot of sweet vermouth, a shot of blended Scotch and a shot of Benedictine. Shake and strain into a glass. Serve with a twist of lemon peel.

50

Most of the **whisky** you buy **already has water in it.** The spirit in the cask contains 50–60% of alcohol by volume (this is the 'cask strength'). The majority of whiskies are then cut (diluted) with distilled water down to about 40–46% by volume. Cask strength whisky is available in special bottlings.

Andrew Langley

Andrew Langley is a knowledgeable food and drink writer. Among his formative influences he lists a season picking grapes in Bordeaux, several years of raising sheep and chickens in Wiltshire and two decades drinking his grandmother's tea. He has written books on a number of Scottish and Irish whisky distilleries and is the editor of the highly regarded anthology of the writings of the legendary Victorian chef Alexis Soyer.

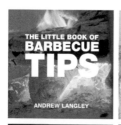

THE LITTLE BOOK OF
BARBECUE TIPS

ANDREW LANGLEY

THE LITTLE BOOK OF
BEER TIPS

ANDREW LANGLEY

THE LITTLE BOOK OF
HERB TIPS

WILLIAM FORTT

THE LITTLE BOOK OF
POKER TIPS

PETER FRENCH

THE LITTLE BOOK OF
GARDENING TIPS

WILLIAM FORTT

THE LITTLE BOOK OF
CHEFS' TIPS

RICHARD MAGGS

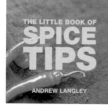

THE LITTLE BOOK OF
SPICE TIPS

ANDREW LANGLEY

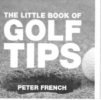

THE LITTLE BOOK OF
GOLF TIPS

PETER FRENCH

THE LITTLE BOOK OF
TIPS SERIES

THE LITTLE BOOK OF
CHEESE TIPS

ANDREW LANGLEY

THE LITTLE BOOK OF
WINE TIPS

ANDREW LANGLEY

THE LITTLE BOOK OF
AGA TIPS²

RICHARD MAGGS

THE LITTLE BOOK OF
COFFEE TIPS

ANDREW LANGLEY

THE LITTLE BOOK OF
TEA TIPS

ANDREW LANGLEY

THE LITTLE BOOK OF
AGA TIPS³

RICHARD MAGGS

THE LITTLE BOOK OF
AGA TIPS

RICHARD MAGGS

THE LITTLE BOOK OF
CHRISTMAS AGA TIPS

RICHARD MAGGS

THE LITTLE BOOK OF
RAYBURN TIPS

RICHARD MAGGS

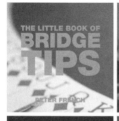

THE LITTLE BOOK OF
BRIDGE
TIPS

PETER FRENCH

THE LITTLE BOOK OF
CHESS
TIPS

PETER FRENCH

THE LITTLE BOOK OF
FISHING
TIPS

MICK DEVENISH

THE LITTLE BOOK OF
GREEN
TIPS

WILLIAM FORTT

THE LITTLE BOOK OF
KITTEN
TIPS

ANDREW LANGLEY

PAUL HARTLEY
THE LITTLE BOOK OF
MARMITE
TIPS

THE LITTLE BOOK OF
PUPPY
TIPS

ANDREW LANGLEY

THE LITTLE BOOK OF
WHISKY
TIPS

ANDREW LANGLEY

THE LITTLE BOOK OF
TRAVEL
TIPS

MEGAN DEVENISH

Little Books of Tips from Absolute Press